PRAGA CAPUT REGNI

© 1995 Flow East RV, Hullenbergweg 379, 1101 CR Amsterdam

Author:
Jaroslav Guth
Marta Trapp

Poems:
Jaroslav Seifert, Nobel Price laureate, translated by Ewald Ozers

© Photographs 1995:
    Josef Ehm, Museum of Decorative Art, Prague
    Jaroslav Guth
    Tibor Honty
    Josef Sudek, Museum of Decorative Art, Prague
    Jindřich Trejbal
    Jaroslav Trnovský
    Vladimír Uher
    Pavel Votruba
    Historical photographs lend by Pavel Scheufler

Edited by Natalie Shashou

Layout:
Ilaria Casalino

Printing and colour separation consultant:
Mara Puccini

Produced by:
Summerfield Press, Florence

Printed in Italy by:
Litografica Faenza

Jaroslav Guth

Poems by Jaroslav Seifert

PRAGA CAPUT REGNI

FLOW EAST

Prague has many names, faces and moods: a city of poetry, art, music, a mecca for visitors and a beloved home for its citizens. Since time immemorial Prague has been praised and admired. Many books have been written about its charm... and now, with respect and love, we add yet another.

Pages 8-9: Panorama of Prague beyond the Vltava River.

Romanesque rotondas:

The Holy Cross in ulice Karolíny Světlé (11th century).

St. Martin at Vyšchrad (11th century).

St. Longin in Na Rybníčku street (12th century).

St. Mary Magdalene at Přední Kopanina (12th century).

Romanesque Hall in the Palace of the Lords of Kunštát in Řetězová street (early 13th century).

A Romanesque column in the Old Palace of the Castle.

A Romanesque foundation of the Old Palace of Prague Castle (10th to 11th centuries).

14

St. Vitus Cathedral, built on the site of a Romanesque church by
Emperor Charles IV (Matthias of Arras and Petr Parléř, 1344-1406).

As I was walking in the fading light -
Prague seemed more beautiful than Rome to me -
I was afraid that from this dream I might
never awake, that I might never see
the stars that, when the daylight comes again,
beneath their folded wings the gargoyles hide-
the gargoyles standing, as on guard, beside
the cornice of St. Vitus' ancient fane.

Interior of St. Vitus Cathedral.

View of Cathedral chancel (started by Matthias of Arras in 1344).

St. Wenceslas Chapel in St. Vitus Cathedral contains semi-precious stones, gold and paintings (Petr Parléř, 1362-1364).

Vladislav Hall (Vladislavský sál), the largest hall in medieval Prague (1486-1502).

View from St. Vitus Cathedral of St. George's Basilica and Monastery, founded in the 10th century.

The romantic Golden Lane (Zlatá ulička) once inhabited by goldsmiths, alchemists and poets. Franz Kafka lived in the little house on the left.

Alley in the Royal Garden, Baroque stone vases by Matyáš
Braun (1729) in the forefront.

The Ball-Game Hall in the Royal Gardens with its unusual
graffiti decoration (1567).

The Ball-Game Hall in the Royal Gardens, detail.

The clatter of the bucket in the well,
a human head behind the dungeon bars-
I happily make for the Belvedere
whose verdigris-green roof winks from afar...

Like a ballerina's pointed slipper
does the spire launch its upward flight;
with candles on the ancient chesnuts
Prague now sparkles, wholly robed in light...

A view of the Royal Summer Palace from Chotkovy sady.

The Royal Garden (Královská zahrada) of the Castle was founded in 1534 in Italian Renaissance style.

View of the Castle from the arcades over the Deer Pit
(Jelení příkop).

View of the Hradčanské náměstí and the Archbishop's Palace from the
first courtyard of the Castle

Capitols of columns from the Černín Palace.

Černín Palace (Francesco Carrati, 1669-1697).

The balconies and porticoes of the Černín Palace were added by Anselm Lurago (1747).

Loreto (facade by Kilián Ignác Diezenhofer, 1720). The famous carillion was constructed by master clockmaker Petr Nauman in 1694.

The Santa Casa (Svatá chýše) and cloisters in Loreto.

The Loreto terrace and stairs with copies of putti.

Steps from Úvoz to Loretánské náměstí.

Kanovnická ulička from Martinic Palace to the New World
(Nový Svět).

The little houses of the New World once inhabited by the alchemists of Emperor Rudolf II.

The New World - a picturesque nook in ancient Hradčany.

Premonstratensian Church of Our Lady (originally of the 12th century, rebuilt in
1743-1751).

The Strahov Monastery of the Premonstratensian Order.

Flight of steps from Pohořelec to the Strahov Monastery.

Philosophical Hall in the Strahov Library, (1782-1784).

Life on the New Castle Steps around 1868.

The New Castle Steps (Nové zámecké schody) built after 1569 to replace a steep carriageway to the Castle.

View of St. Nicholas Church (Sv. Mikuláše) from the New Castle Steps.

Sleep, town of pantiled roofs and roaming cats,
return your weapons to your armoury !
Two lovers walk across the ancient bridge,
a silent bird regards them from a tree.

The Old Castle Steps (Staré zámecké schody).

Roofs of the Lesser Quarter in Nerudova ulice.

42

House signs in Nerudova Street:
The Red Lamb,
The Three Violins,
The Key,
The Two Suns,
The Golden Goblet.

View of Nerudova ulice and the Lesser Quarter from the Town Hall Steps (Radniční schody).

Spring in Prague comes on kittens' paws,
slinking over pantiles black with smoke.
Leaning on a parapet I gaze
as over roofs and cornice hangs a haze
of shimmering white cherry blossom.
But total happiness cannot be mine
unless at least I hear the whispering weir
through air as light as sacramental wine.

Romantic spots a few steps from Nerudova Street.

St. Nicholas Church by Kryštof and Kilián Ignác Diezenhofer is the
most beautiful building in Czech Baroque (1704-1755).

Nocturnal view of St. Nicholas Church from Mostecká ulice.

Statue inside of St. Nicholas Church.

The interior of the dome of St. Nicholas Church.

St. Nicholas Church choir and organ, which Mozart used to play.

The vision of St. Hubert (Ferdinand Maxmilián Brokoff, 1726) seen on an important Baroque house, "The Golden Stag".

Typical nook in the Lesser Quarter.

Baroque guard-stones in front of Lobkovic Palace in the Lesser Quarter.

Even under bombs and heavy shelling
I'd write a sonnet undeterred--
but 'midst a springtime shower of blossoms
I could not write a single word.

And when the weirs on Prague's old river
like peals of girlish laughter ring--
yes, then my pen drops from my fingers
and I am wholly drunk with spring.

Charm and beauty in the ancient streets of the Lesser
Quarter.

Velkopřevorské náměstí with the large Buquoy Palace.   Night scene in the Lesser Quarter.

56

The Infant Jesus of Prague, 16th century, is especially famous in Latin America.

Beethoven, Mozart and other celebrities stayed at the famous "Golden Unicorn Hotel" (U zlatého jednorožce) on Maltézské náměstí.

Church of Our Lady below the Chain (kostel P. Marie pod řetězem) belonging to the Knights of Malta, is the residence of the Grand Prior. Gothic spires express the knightly and militant character of the Order.

Sala terrena and the avenue of statues by Adrian de Vries in the Wallenstein Garden.

The Wallenstcin Garden (Valdštenská zahrada) of the palace of the Imperial Marshall Albrecht of Wallenstein (1624-1630).

A radiant day. So difficult to leave
a shrub about to bloom.
My Prague, you lovely flowergirl,
why should I leave you now?

I greet you, city, if one may
greet stone as it deserves:
My Prague, you lovely flowergirl,
vendor of gold and curves.

A delightful view of St. Nicholas Church from Vrtba Garden (Vrtbovská zahrada).

Steps from Vrbta Garden (statues and vases from Matyáš Braun's workshop, circa 1725).

The Kolovrat Garden (Kolovratská zahrada), founded circa 1785.

Steps and arbour in Kolovrat Garden, the most beautiful garden below Prague Castle.

The watermills stand all along the river
but now their idle wheels are unemployed:
a cheeky wind whistles its vernal joys
as, with the tripping step of barefoot boys,
spring gilds the statues on the bridge.

This is part of The Devil's Stream known as the "Venice of Prague".

The Devil's Stream (Čertovka) mill race separates Kampa from the Lesser Quarter.

View of Charles Bridge (Karlův Most) from Kampa.

Traditional potters' market in Kampa in 1910.

Kampa in winter.

The millwheel now is dry and rotten,
those serenades are long forgotten
that it played in younger days.
The happy river, though--you know it,
is youthful for the thousandth time,
tuning its strings for song and rhyme.

View from Kampa of the Novotného Footbridge (Novotného lávka) and
Old Town Mills (Staroměstské mlýny).

View from Kampa of the Vltava River and the National Theatre.

Over this bridge so full of glory
and sadness I am fond of strolling;
where severed human heads were rolling
a band now plays its repertory.

Over this bridge some time in April
spring overnight invades our city,
and to the sound of drums and trumpets
young girls lose their viriginity
or do some things that are unwise,
as by the weir above the waters
a hundred seagulls dip and rise.

The Vltava River with the Charles Bridge gives the most fascinating views of Prague.

Charles Bridge illuminated in the winter.

Křižík's electric tram on Charles Bridge (28 September 1905).

An evening mood on Charles Bridge

View from Charles Bridge of the Lesser Quarter Bridge Tower and the Castle.

Charles Bridge in all its glory.

An enchanting morning on Charles Bridge.

Charles Bridge, 14th century, is unique. There is no lovlier bridge in the world (the Baroque statues 1683-1714).

Life on the banks of the Vltava River under Charles Bridge.

Fisherman under Charles Bridge in the morning.

The statues on the Tower represent Charles IV as Holy Roman Emperor and Wenceslas IV as the Roman King, between them stands St. Vitus, the patron saint of Charles Bridge.

The Old Town Bridge Tower is the most beautiful fortification structure in Central Europe (Petr Parléř, 1380-1400).

Detail of sculptural ornament on the Tower.

Prague, whose beauty cannot be encompassed
even by a firmament of stars...
Standing, robed in radiance cap-à-pie,
from her antlers' towers hung a cross-
and a hunstman sank upon his knee,
unable to raise his bow again.

Prague, whose beauty cannot be encompassed
by human words that tremble on the lip:
see, your poets wander through your alleys
but instead of writing verse they weep.

Křižovnické náměstí is the most beautiful square in the Old Town. The Church of
the Knights of the Cross is on the left, St. Salvátor Church in the foreground.

View of Prague Castle over the spires near Križovnické
námestí and Karlova ulice.

The Clementinum - formerly a Jesuit College - is the largest complex of buildings after Prague Castle.

The Mirror Chapel of the Clementinum (1724).

Karlova Ulice and the Italian Chapel (1590-1600).

The remarkable lattice gate of the Italian Chapel.

An 1885 view of Karlova ulice and the "Blue Pike House" which King Wenceslas IV and his executioner used to frequent.

In 1701 statues of saints were added to the Renaissance house of the "Golden Well" as protection against the plague.

Traditional market on the Old Town Square (Staroměstské náměstí) in 1910.

An Old Town Renaissance window with the inscription PRAGA CAPUT REGNI (Praha Matka Měst).

The Old Town Hall with the clock by Master Hanuš, and a Gothic oriel bay window (14th to 16th centuries).

King George of Poděbrady Hall with remnants of Gothic and Renaissance frescoes.

Old Town Hall: ceremonial entrance, a mosaic from a sketch by Mikuláš Aleš was added in 1937.

View of Týn Church from the Old Town Hall tower.

Jan Hus monument in front of the Týn Church.

97

View from Týn of the Old Town Square and Hradčany.

The tombstone of Danish astronomer Tycho de Brahe in Týn Church (1601).

The Gothic arcade in front of Tyn was erected during the reign of Wenceslas IV to shelter merchants from bad weather.

The Old Town Church of St. Nicholas (Kilián Ignác Dienzenhofer, 1732-1735).

Interior of St. Nicholas Church.

Reliefs and statues on the facade of St. Nicholas Church.

A wrought iron Renaissance fountain on the Little Square (Malý rynek).

View of Ungelt and St. James Church from a Tyn Tower. The 11th century, Ungelt was a centre for merchants as well as the customs house of the Bohemian kings.

The "Two Golden Bears", the Renaissance house in which the famous "zealous" reporter Egon Erwin Kisch was born in 1885.

The statue of Moses in front of the Old-New Synagogue (Staronová synagoga, sculptor František Bílek).

The Gothic Old-New Synagogue, 14th century, and the Renaissance Jewish Town Hall.

This is where the famous scholar and magician Rabbi Löw was laid to rest (died in 1609).

Pages 108-109: The Jewish Cemetery in Prague is world renowned.

107

The Jewish ghetto was once a labyrinth of narrow streets with shockingly bad housing. The quarter was demolished around 1896 and only the Cemetery, Town Hall and Synagogue remain.

Franz Kafka spent his youth in this environment.

The irreparable errors made during the demolition of the Jewish ghetto gave rise to a strong movement for the rescue of old Prague, and so large parts of the city have been preserved.

View of St. Giles Church (14th century) from Husova ulice, one of the oldest streets in Prague (12th century).

Statues of giants and decorations on the portal of Clam-Gallas Palace (Matyáš Braun, 1714).

The Bethlehem Chapel (Betlémská kaple) where Jan Hus preached from 1402 to 1414.

The Convent of the Blessed Agnes (Klášter sv. Anežky České) at František, built by Kings Wenceslas I and Přemysl II in 1234-1280. This complex is the first Gothic monument in Bohemia.

The Carolinium is the seat of the oldest university in Central Europe, founded by Emperor Charles IV in 1348.

A 1900 photograph shows the Powder Tower as it was before ulice Na příkopě was rebuilt, and before the art nouveau Municipal House (Obecní dům) was built.

The Powder Tower (Prašná brána), built as a gate to the Old Town and a part of its fortifications is at the end of ulice Na příkopě.

A 1905 photograph shows the Nostic Theatre and its surroundings, which is almost as it was when Don Giovanni had its first night in 1787.

Mozart stayed at the "Three Lions" as guest of Dušek and his wife. He had a view of the Nostic Theatre from his window.

Mozart composed "Don Giovanni" at the Bertramka farm: this photograph from 1875 is said to be the same as it was in Mozart's day.

The vineyard farmstead of Bertramka is now the Museum of Mozart and of farm's owner, the composer František Dušek.

Wenceslas Square in 1876.

Wenceslas Square with the National Museum and the statue of St. Wenceslas, patron of Bohemia, at its upper end is the scene of much of the modern history of the Czech nation.

The lower end of Wenceslas Square (Václavské náměstí) around 1880 and today.

An 1868 photograph shows the former Chain Bridge (Řetězový most) and the Castle with the incomplete St. Vitus Cathedral (completed in 1873-1929).

The National Theatre was the highpoint of 19th century Czech architecture. Bedřich Smetana composed his famous opera "The Bartered Bride" in Lažanský Palace opposite the theatre.

The Pantheon at Vyšehrad Cemetery commemorates the most illustrious figures of the Czech nation.

The arcades of Vyšehrad Cemetery over the tombs of famous persons, such as composer Antonín Dvořák.

From the 10th century Vyšehrad was the second Prague residence of the Bohemian princes. It stands on a rock which closes the Prague valley to the south.

Everywhere they dug for gold
Prague, though hundreds of years old,
robes herself in white in springtime.
More bewitched than any man can
be I fling my window open:
all is lace as in a cancan.

A view from Petřín hill of St. Nicholas Church.

Petřín hill in Spring.

128

Statues in Prague gardens and parks (John the Baptist by Auguste Rodin and Pomona by Aristide Maillol).

Villa America, a summer residence of Jan Michna of Vacínov (Kilián Ignác Diezenhofer, 1712-1720).

The interior of Villa America - now the Antonín Dvořák Museum.

The Baroque interior of the sanctuary - Church of our Lady Victorious - on the White Mountain.

A sanctuary for pilgrimage on the White Mountain (Bílá hora).

The Late Baroque Church of St. Margaret in the Břevnov monastery (Kryštof Dienzenhofer, 1708-1714).

The Romanesque foundations of the Břevnov monastery.

The first monastery in Bohemia - the Benedictine Monastery at Břevnov - founded by St. Adalbert and Prince Boleslav I in 993.

Trója Chateau - the Early Baroque villa of Count Václav Vojtěch of Štemberk (1679-1685).

The inside of the balustrade is formed by a dramatic battle between Gods and Titans.

The balustrade of Trója Chateau with its gallery of statues leading to its large garden.

The garden of the chateau with its terraces and ceramic vases is the first French-style park in Bohemia (1700).

The style of life, art and architecture known as Art Nouveau was represented in
Prague by:
Grand Hotel Evropa,
Main Railway Station,
Municipal House.

142

143

The famous "U Fleků" has been brewing a special dark beer for centuries.

It is always pleasant to stop in one of the many Prague restaurants or pubs.

Hašek's "Good Soldier Schweik" made the restaurant "U Kalicha" famous.

The garden restaurant in Stromovka, Prague's largest park.

An attracticc café and restaurant is Hanavský Pavilion in Letná Park above the Vltava.
Hanavský Pavilion is a Neo-Baroque structure of Czech cast iron, originally built for the 1891 Industrial Jubilee Exhibition.

From the Pavilion there is a magnificent view of the Vltava and its bridges.
No other river and city blend together in the manner of Prague and the Vltava.

And all your towers, like the pipes
of a Gothic organ,
at nightfall play to the lighted streetlamps
a requiem for Europe.

This then is Prague, my city and my love,
my hope and armour, pledge against defeat:
a heart that should have stopped a hundred times,
yet beats, and beats, and beats with fevered heat.

BLUE PRAHA
M&J Genuine Design a.s.
Malé náměstí 14, Praha 1
tel.: 242 16 717